My Choices

By

Grace Jones

©2017
Book Life
King's Lynn
Norfolk PE30 4LS

ISBN: 978-1-78637-174-4

Written by:
Grace Jones

Designed by:
Evie Wright

A catalogue record for this book
is available from the British Library

Photo Credits

**Abbreviations: l-left, r-right, b-bottom,
t-top, c-centre, m-middle.**

Front cover – Rawpixel.com. 2 – Pressmaster. 4 – Rawpixel.com.
5 – Pressmaster. 6 – Ronnachai Palas. 7 – Amelaxa. 8 – Poznyakov. 9 – Anna
Om. 10 – FamVeld. 11 – Sergey Novikov. 12 – Monkey Business Images.
13 – Lyubov Kobyakova . 14 – Sunabesyou 15 – Martin Novak. 16 – Tatyana Vyc.
17 – ITALO. 18 – Szasz-Fabian Jozsef. 19 – ESB Professional. 20 – Zurijeta.
21 – Szefei. 22 – Madrolly. 23 – Imtmphoto.
Images are courtesy of Shutterstock.com. With thanks to Getty Images,
Thinkstock Photo and iStockphoto.

Contents

Words that look like **this** can be found in the glossary on page 24.

What Are Choices?

Every day, people from all over the world make lots of different choices.

Choices are the decisions people make between one thing and another.

I'm cycling to school today.

Some of the choices that you make will only affect you, like choosing what clothes to wear.

Why Are Choices Important?

I helped my sister to make a sandcastle.

Making choices allows you to do the things that make you happy.

Being able to make choices means that we can choose who our friends are.

Good Choices

It is important that we make the right choices because our choices can also affect others.

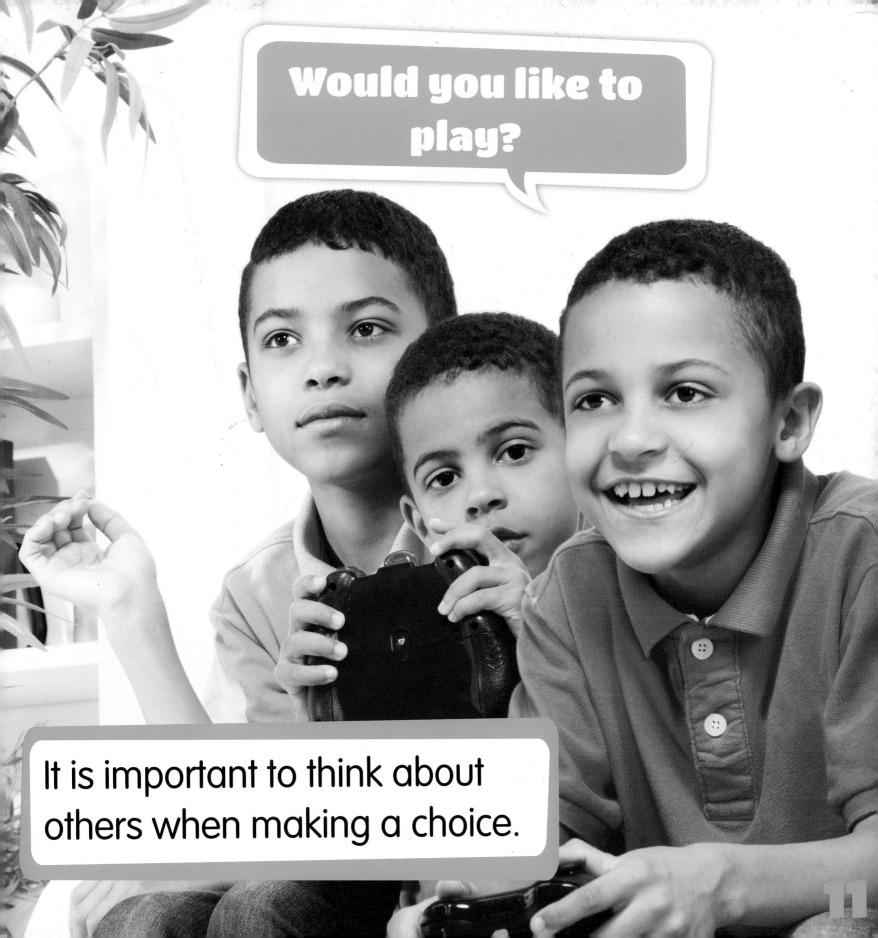

Would you like to play?

It is important to think about others when making a choice.

11

Drew's parents asked him to eat his dinner instead of going out to play with his friends.

Drew made the choice to eat his dinner to keep his parents happy. This was a good choice.

Difficult Choices

Sometimes choices are very easy to make. Other choices are much more difficult to make.

It is important that we choose to do things that are **respectful**.

I love to ice skate.

Steffi wanted to go ice skating but her brother wanted her to watch him play football.

I'm so happy my sister came!

Steffi chose to watch her brother play football as she knew that it would make him happy.

At School

Can I help you to carry your books?

It is important to behave and make the right choices at school.

If you make the right choices, you may become a **role model** for other children.

At Home

Can I help you to wash the plates?

It is important to help your parents and make the right choices at home.

If you make good choices, you may become a good role model for your **siblings**.

Other People's Choices

Sometimes you might not like the choices that other people make.

Don't put your rubbish on the floor!

If someone else's choice upsets you, talk to a parent or teacher about what has happened.

Glossary

respectful to consider the feelings, wishes and rights of other people

role model someone who shows others how to behave

siblings brothers and sisters

Index